Using Your Language Series

Grammar Handbook

for

Home and School

by Carl B. Smith, Ph.D.

GRAYSON BERNARD
P U B L I S H E R S

Book design by Kathleen McConahay and
　Addie Seabarkrob
Cover design by Addie Seabarkrob

Library of Congress Cataloging-in-Publication Data

Smith, Carl Bernard.
　Grammar handbook for home and school / by Carl B. Smith.
　p. cm. -- (Using your language series)
　Summary: Presents basic principles of English grammar and
punctuation with definitions of terms and examples of proper
usage.
　ISBN 0–9628556–7–7 : $8.95
　1. English language--Grammar--1950- --Juvenile literature.
[1. English language--Grammar.] I. Title. II. Series: Smith, Carl
Bernard. Using your language series.
PE1112.S548　1992　　　428.2--dc20　　　92-19371

Grayson Bernard Publishers
223 S. Pete Ellis Drive, Suite 12
Post Office Box 5247
Bloomington, Indiana 47407

About the author:

Carl B. Smith, Ph.D. is professor of education at Indiana University in Bloomington, founder and director of the Family Literacy Center, and director of the ERIC Clearinghouse on Reading and Communication Skills. He is a former classroom teacher and reading specialist, and a longtime author of the Macmillan Reading Program.

Also by Carl B. Smith:

Intermediate Grammar: A Student's Resource Book

Expand Your Child's Vocabulary: A Twelve-Week Plan

Elementary Grammar: A Child's Resource Book

Help Your Child Read and Succeed: A Parents' Guide

A Commitment to Critical Thinking

Teacher as Decision-Maker

Contents

Acknowledgments

Eugene Reade's research and guidance on this book give me a sense of security in its content. His quick eye and his sure-footed logic always enhance a person's writing.

The editorial and design staff of Grayson Bernard kept me on target and arranged the clean, easy-to-use format that pleases the eye and makes this the efficient guidebook it should be. My many thanks to Kathleen McConahay, Addie Seabarkrob, and Susan Yerolemou.

Carl B. Smith

Introduction

Your concern for improving grammar and punctuation shows that you are interested in clear, direct communication. The guidelines and examples in this book will help you speak and write more clearly than the average person. By following these accepted principles of grammar and punctuation, you will be able to formulate straightforward sentences that help your listener or reader understand the point you want to make.

Students always have questions about word usage, sentence structure, and punctuation. Today, they often must find the answers for themselves because many schools no longer teach grammar and punctuation in a formal way. They are encouraged to use handbooks and to ask others for help. Parents can assist their children by showing them how to use this book. If children learn to consult this handbook on a regular basis, they will quickly learn how to answer their own questions about grammar and punctuation, and they will feel secure in knowing that their language conforms to standard usage.

1) Therefore, use this book as a quick reference source.

2) Follow the alphabetical listing to find information about the most frequently used terms in grammar and punctuation.

3) Look at the sentences that are provided to illustrate each definition and guideline.

Sometimes you may want explanations and examples that are more extensive than those given in this brief *Grammar Handbook*. You can find this information in *Intermediate Grammar: A Student's Resource Book* by Carl B. Smith. In that book you will find many examples of clear sentences, and you will see how to correct errors in actual compositions written by students in the intermediate grades. You will also find exercises that help you to check your understanding.

Keep a copy of this *Grammar Handbook* wherever students do their schoolwork, and refer to *Intermediate Grammar* whenever you need more help. Use them to help you achieve your goal of clear communication in everything you say and write.

- **Adjectives** are words that modify nouns or pronouns.

When we *modify* a word, we make its meaning more specific by adding other words that tell more about it.

Articles are the adjectives *a*, *an*, and *the*.

The articles *a* and *an* are singular and refer to any person or thing.

▼ Use *a* before words beginning with a consonant.
There was *a* bad storm last night.

▼ Use *an* before words beginning with a vowel.
They ate *an* enormous pizza.

The article *the* refers to a specific thing or things. *The* is used before singular or plural nouns.

The waves were pounding against *the* shore.

Adjective suffixes are word endings which let us know that a word is being used as an adjective. These are some of the adjective suffixes used most often:

-*ous*: famous, nervous, enormous
-*y*: happy, lazy, funny
-*ful*: hopeful, useful, beautiful
-*ish*: foolish, childish, selfish
-*ic*: basic, heroic, authentic
-*ive*: active, expensive, aggressive
-*able*: usable, probable, available
-*less*: worthless, hopeless, useless

Comparisons can often be made by changing the endings of adjectives.

The **positive form** of the adjective is used to modify one thing: *small, large.* This is the form of the adjective before endings are added.

The **comparative form** is used to compare two things. Most adjectives add *er* in the comparative form: *smaller, larger.*

The **superlative form** is used to compare more than two things. Most adjectives add *est* in the superlative form: *smallest, largest.*

▼ When an adjective ends with a short vowel followed by a single consonant, this final consonant should be doubled before adding *er* and *est*.
   big, bigger, biggest

▼ When an adjective ends with *y*, this *y* is changed to *i* before *er* or *est* are added.
   funny, funnier, funniest

▼ When an adjective ends with *e*, this letter is dropped before *er* and *est* are added.
   wide, wider, widest

▼ When an adjective contains a **vowel digraph** (such as *ou* or *ai*) in the final syllable, there is no change in the spelling of the base word when inflections are added.
   loud, louder, loudest   plain, plainer, plainest

▼ If an adjective ends with two consonants, no change is made in the base word when *er* and *est* are added.
   cold, colder, coldest   fresh, fresher, freshest

If an adjective contains any kind of digraph (vowel or consonant) in the final syllable, do not change the spelling when you add endings.

Comparisons using *more* and *most* are made with adjectives of more than one syllable to show an *increase* in size, degree, or quantity.

- Use the word ***more*** for the comparative form of adjectives containing more than one syllable: *more important.*
- Use the word ***most*** for the superlative form of adjectives containing more than one syllable: *most important.*

Comparisons using *less* and *least* are made with adjectives of more than one syllable to show a *decrease* in size, degree, or quantity.

- Use the word *less* for the comparative form of adjectives containing more than one syllable: *less important.*
- Use the word *least* for the superlative form of adjectives containing more than one syllable: *least important.*

Irregular adjectives have special comparative and superlative forms:

good, better, best
bad, worse, worst
far, farther, farthest
some, more, most
many, more, most
much, more, most
little, less, least

Be careful with *worse*, which compares only two things, and *worst*, which compares more than two.

This pizza is *worse* than that one. The pizza we had yesterday was the *worst* I ever ate.

Adjectives in a series are handled in the following ways:

▼ When there are *only* two adjectives in a series, they can often be used without any separation between them if they work together to modify the noun.

They live in the **little white** house on the corner.

▼ When two nouns are of *equal importance* and modify the noun in different ways, they should be separated by a comma.

He is a **talented, accomplished** performer.

If the order of the two adjectives could be reversed, or if the word *and* could be used between the two adjectives, then they should also be separated by a comma.

He is an **accomplished, talented** performer.
He is a **talented and accomplished** performer.

▼ Whenever *more* than two adjectives are used in a series, they should be separated by commas .

It was a **cold, dark, windy** day.

Proper adjectives are derived from proper nouns. Proper adjectives are always capitalized.

The **California** condor is a large vulture.
We had some **Wisconsin** cheese and **Georgia** peaches.

Sometimes it is necessary to change the ending of a proper noun to form a proper adjective. Some proper adjectives end with *-an* or *-ian*, and others end with *-ish* or *-ese*.

Proper Noun	Proper Adjective
America	American
Mexico	Mexican
Canada	Canadian
Italy	Italian
England	English
Denmark	Danish
China	Chinese
Japan	Japanese

Demonstrative adjectives indicate exactly which people or things we are talking about.

Singular	Plural
this	these
that	those

This and *these* refer to people or things that are nearby or have just been mentioned.

This movie is really terrible.
I hope *these* alligators have been fed recently.

That and *those* refer to people or things that are some distance away or were referred to in the past.

That stream is deeper than it looks.
Those elephants seem to be headed this way.

Predicate adjectives follow linking verbs and modify the subject of the sentence. These adjectives appear in the predicate of the sentence and give more information about nouns or pronouns in the subject.

This book is very **interesting.**

He was **alone** and **afraid.**

When more than two predicate adjectives are used, commas separate each pair of adjectives. Also, a word such as *and* is used before the last adjective in the series.

The day was **cold, dark, *and* windy**.

ADVERBS

> • **Adverbs** are words that modify verbs, adjectives, or other adverbs.

The suffix -ly is used at the end of many adverbs. A *suffix* is a syllable added to the end of a word to change the way the word is used. In many cases, we can add -*ly* to the end of an adjective to change it to an adverb.

Adjective	Adverb
slow	slowly
safe	safely
easy	easily
careful	carefully

Intensifiers are adverbs that tell *how much*. They are often used before adjectives or other adverbs to add greater emphasis to the words they modify. The adverb *very* is probably the most frequently used intensifier. Here are a few others:

too	extremely
nearly	completely
quite	definitely
really	entirely

This box is **too** *heavy* to carry.
We were **completely** *exhausted* after the long walk.

Comparisons can be made with adverbs, just as they can with adjectives.

▼ Adverbs in the **positive degree** give the basic form of the word. These adverbs modify a single verb, adjective, or adverb.
Charles ran **fast** to get out of the rain.
The train chugged **slowly** up the mountain.

▼ Adverbs in the **comparative degree** are used to compare two things. Some adverbs can add -er in the comparative degree.
Louis can run **faster** than I can.

When adverbs contain two or more syllables, and especially when they end with -ly, the comparative degree is formed by adding the word *more* before the adverb.
Your turtle walks **more slowly** than mine.

▼ Adverbs in the **superlative degree** are used to compare more than two things. Some adverbs can add -est in the superlative degree.
She swims the **fastest** of anyone on the team.
Most adverbs of two or more syllables form the superlative degree by adding *most* before the adverb.
My snail crawls **most slowly** of all.

The following adverbs have their own patterns:

Positive	Comparative	Superlative
well	better	best
badly	worse	worst
far	farther	farthest
little	less	least

Some words can be adjectives or adverbs. This is determined by the kind of verb that is used in the sentence. *Well* is often used as both parts of speech. *Well* is an adjective when it is used with a linking verb. It describes what the subject *is,* not what it does.

He is **well**. She feels **well**.

Well is an adverb when it is used with an action verb. It describes *how* the action of the verb is performed.

She swims **well**. He hit the ball **well**.

A number of other words can be adjectives or adverbs: *hard, high, low, early,* and *late,* for example.

This bench is very **hard**. (adjective)

We worked **hard** all day. (adverb)

Double negatives appear when two negative words are used in the same sentence. If you make a negative statement using the adverb *not* after the verb, then there should be no other negative words in the sentence. Negative words include *no, none, never, nobody,* and *nothing.*

The next two sentences contain double negatives:

I **do not** have *no* idea where he is.
I **didn't** know *nobody* at the dance.

Here is the correct way to write these sentences:

I **do not** have *any* idea where he is.
I **didn't** know *anybody* at the dance.

ANTONYMS

> • **Antonyms** are words that have opposite meanings.

big - little   inside - outside
close - open   sad - happy
wet - dry   over - under
light - dark   left - right
on - off   front - back
stop - start   yes - no
come - go   then - now
high - low   far - near
first - last   lost - found

CLAUSES

> • **Clauses** are groups of words that contain a subject and a predicate.

▼ An **independent clause** is complete and makes sense by itself.
We decided to go back home.

▼ A **dependent clause** is *not* complete and does not make sense by itself.
Because the weather was very bad . . .

The subordinating conjunction *because* makes this clause incomplete. It will make sense only when it is combined with an independent clause:

Because the weather was very bad, we decided to go back home.
We decided to go back home *because the weather was very bad*.

See the section on **Sentences** in this Handbook to find out more about how clauses are used.

CONJUNCTIONS

> • **Conjunctions** are function words that join two or more words, phrases, or clauses.

Function words (or *structure words*) do not name things or express actions, but they are important because they make connections between vocabulary words.

Coordinating conjunctions can be used to connect other words such as nouns or verbs. They can also be used to show the relationship between parts of the sentence. When we *coordinate* things, we cause them to work well *together*. Often the things that we coordinate are of equal importance within the sentence.

The words *and*, *but*, and *or* are the most frequently used coordinating conjunctions.

- *And* can be used to join words or groups of words.
  Bill **and** *I* are on the same team.
  We *practice* after school **and** *play* on Saturdays.
- *And* can also connect the parts of a *compound sentence*.
  The parade begins at noon, **and** the game starts at one.
- *And* can be used to connect words in a series.
  We found old shoes **and** hats **and** junk in the attic.

12

The coordinating conjunctions *but* and *or* show other kinds of connections between words.

- *But* is used to show *contrast*.
  We felt tired **but** happy when the trip was over.
  The package was small **but** very heavy.

- *Or* is used to show that there is a *choice* between different things.
  You can have chocolate **or** strawberry ice cream.
  Mom **or** dad should know when you're coming back.

The words *yet, for,* and *nor* can also be used as coordinating conjunctions.

The car was old and rusty, **yet** it ran very well.
They will probably succeed, **for** they have worked hard and prepared well.
I haven't seen him today, **nor** do I expect to see him tomorrow.

Subordinating conjunctions connect the main part of a sentence with another part that serves as a modifier. The words following the subordinating conjunction make sense only in relation to the main part of the sentence.

Here are some subordinating conjunctions that are often used:

after	though
although	unless
as	until
because	when
before	whenever
if	where
since	wherever
than	while

We left **before** *the movie ended.*
The game was stopped **because** *the rain started.*

Correlative conjunctions are always used in pairs. They show the relationship between one part of a sentence and another part of the sentence. The word *correlate* means "to show a connection between things" or "to show how things are to be used together."

Here are the most frequently used correlative conjunctions:

if . . . then
both . . . and
either . . . or
neither . . . nor
not only . . . but also

Both my uncle **and** my cousin came to visit.
Either finish the job **or** let someone else do it.
He lost **not only** his wallet **but also** his keys.

If you use the first part of a correlative conjunction, *then* you must follow it with the second part of the pattern.

- **Contractions** are shortened forms that join two words into one. In a contraction, some letters in one of the words are omitted and are replaced by an apostrophe (').

Many contractions involve a verb followed by the word *not*. Other contractions involve a noun or a subject pronoun followed by forms of the verbs *be*, *have*, or *will*.

▼ When a verb is followed by the word *not*, an apostrophe can take the place of the *o* in *not*. The shortened form (*n't*) is joined to the verb to form a contraction.
> I **don't** know when he will be back.
> (I **do not** know when he will be back.)

▼ The words *will not* can be shortened to *won't*.
> We **won't** be able to finish on time.
> (We **will not** be able to finish on time.)

▼ The verbs *be*, *have*, and *will* can be contracted when they follow subject pronouns: *I'm*, *he's*, *we're*, *I've*, *you'd*, *she'll*, *we'll*, and so on.

▼ The word *would* can be written as the contraction *'d*.
> **I'd** like to meet them.
> (I **would** like to meet them.)

▼ It is also possible to use contractions to join verbs to nouns.

This **car's** in bad shape.
(This **car is** in bad shape.)
That **kite'll** never fly.
(That **kite will** never fly.)

FUNCTION WORDS

Function words (or structure words) do not name things or express actions. However, they are important because they make connections and show relationships among other words and parts of the sentence. The two most important types of function words are **conjunctions** and **prepositions**.

- **Conjunctions** are used to join two or more words, phrases, or clauses.

The most frequently used conjunctions are *and, but,* and *or*. (See the separate entry for **Conjunctions** in this Handbook.)

Ellen **and** I are going to a movie.
We had lots of fun on vacation, **but** we were glad to get back home.
Give the message to Roy **or** Carlos.

- **Prepositions** are used to show how *nouns* or *pronouns* are related to other words in the sentence.

Some frequently used prepositions are *to, for, at, with,* and *in.* (See the separate entry for **Prepositions** in this Handbook.)

> We went **to** a movie.
> This package is **for** you.
> We met them **at** the gym.

* **Homographs** are words that have the same *spelling* but have different meanings and belong to different parts of speech. Sometimes their pronunciation also changes even though spelling remains the same.

The polar *bear* is a very large animal. (noun)
This little truck cannot *bear* any more weight. (verb)

That precious stone was almost *perfect.* (adjective)
Athletes *perfect* their skills after years of practice. (verb)

The strong *wind* did a lot of damage. (noun)
The cat helped me *wind* all this yarn into a ball. (verb)

HOMOPHONES

- **Homophones** (also called *homonyms*) are words that have the same *sound* but have different spellings and meanings.

Are you going *to* the game on Saturday?
No, I've got *too* much work to do.
Well, I have *two* tickets if you change your mind.

There is the wallet I lost last week.
They found *their* car keys under the sofa.
They're glad that the long trip is over.

It's really hot today!
The town is very proud of *its* new garbage truck.

There's an enormous *hole* in my new shirt!
He ate the *whole* pizza and didn't give us any!

INTERJECTIONS

- **Interjections** are words that are "thrown" into a conversation for added emphasis or to express strong feelings of surprise: *Ouch*; *Ah*; *Wow*; *Hey*.
- Interjections do not affect sentence structure.

Interjections are often used before a complete sentence and are followed by an exclamation mark.

> *Hey!* Don't leave without me!
> *Ouch!* That really hurt!
> *Good grief!* Hasn't he finished yet?
> *Oh, NO!* I just broke my new watch!

Interjections may also be used at the beginning of a sentence, followed by a comma. This makes the effect much milder than the preceding examples.

> *Well*, I told you so.
> *Aha*, that's what I thought!

- **Nouns** are words that name people, places, or things. Nouns can also name animals, actions, events, times, ideas, or groups of things.

Nouns are often used in their **base** forms.

A **base word** is the form of the word as it is spelled before endings are added or any other changes are made. The base form gives the essential meaning of the noun: *dog*, *car*, *tree*, *house*, for example.

Singular nouns name one person, place or thing: *boy, girl, city, school, table, bus.* Singular nouns are usually base words.

Collective nouns name *groups* or collections that contain several individual people or things.

A **crowd** of people . . .
A **herd** of elephants . . .
A **bunch** of flowers . . .

Concrete nouns name specific people or things that can be seen or touched: *friend, book, tree, chair.*

Abstract nouns name ideas, qualities, or emotions that *cannot* be seen or touched: *truth, honesty, joy.*

Compound nouns are made up of two or more other words. Often the shorter words are nouns in their base forms.

▼ **Closed compounds** are joined without any break:
football   mailbox

▼ **Hyphenated compounds** connect words with a hyphen (-).
front-runner   baby-sitter

▼ **Open compounds** are written as separate words.
high school   ice cream

Inflections are alterations which show that there has been a change in the way a word is used. Inflections are used to change nouns from singular to plural. Often an inflection involves the addition of letters at the end of a base word (*book, books*). Some inflections affect the spelling in other ways (*man, men*).

Plural nouns name two or more people or places or things.

▼ Most nouns form the plural by adding the inflection *s* at the end of the singular noun.
car, cars   table, tables

▼ Singular nouns that end with *s, ss, x, sh, ch*, or *z* add the inflection *es* to form the plural.
bus, buses   class, classes
box, boxes   reflex, reflexes
dish, dishes   ditch, ditches
whiz, whizzes   buz, buzzes

▼ Singular nouns that end with a **consonant** and the letter *y* change the *y* to *i* before adding *es*.
baby, babies   lady, ladies
fly, flies   puppy, puppies

▼ Singular nouns that end with *ie* or with a **vowel and the letter** *y* simply add *s* to form the plural.

tie, ties	movie, movies
boy, boys	key, keys
day, days	valley, valleys

Irregular nouns do not add *s* or *es* in the plural. These nouns change the vowel or use other endings in the plural.

man, men	person, people
woman, women	child, children

Common nouns name *any* person, place, or thing: *boy, girl, town, chair.*

Proper nouns identify *specific* people, places, or things. **Proper nouns are always capitalized:** *William Shakespeare, Paris, Statue of Liberty.*

Possessive nouns show ownership. Possessive nouns end with inflections that involve the **apostrophe** (').

▼ **Singular possessive nouns** are usually formed by adding an apostrophe and *s* (**'s**) to the singular noun.
My **brother's** junk is all over the place.

If the singular noun ends with *s* or *ss*, then the possessive can be formed by the apostrophe alone. This is usually done when the noun has two or more syllables and the following word also begins with the /s/ sound.

The **actress'** story was in all the papers.

▼ **Plural possessive nouns** usually add only the apostrophe to plural nouns that already end with *s* or *es*.

> Both of their **dogs'** collars were worn out.
> The **boxes'** labels were hard to read.

For irregular plural nouns that do not end with *s* or *es*, add **'s** to form the possessive.

> The **women's** hats are on the shelf.
> All of the **children's** coats were in the closet.

Nouns in a series result when two or more nouns are used one after the other.

▼ When two nouns are used in a series, they are usually joined by *and* or *or*.

> Snakes *and* lizards were crawling on the rocks.
> Bill *or* Ed will give you a ride.

▼ When three or more nouns are used in a series, they should be separated by commas. A word such as *and* or *or* should come before the last noun in the series.

> Dozens of **cars, trucks, trailers, and buses** were caught in the snowstorm.
> All of my **books, papers, and pencils** are in the car.

PARTS OF SPEECH

> • The **parts of speech** are the categories into which words are grouped. These categories indicate the way in which words are used in sentences.

The most important parts of speech are these:

Noun	Adverb
Pronoun	Preposition
Verb	Conjunction
Adjective	

You will find all of these parts of speech listed as main entries in this Handbook (**ADJECTIVE, ADVERB** and so on).

One other part of speech is the *interjection.* Interjections are words such as *Oops, Wow, Gosh,* and *Ouch.* These words are used only to give added emphasis; they do not affect the structure of the sentence.

> Ouch! I just mashed my finger.
> Wow, did you see that?

- **Prefixes** are syllables added to the *beginning* of words: **un***lock*, **dis***like*, **re***play*.

Prefixes change the *meaning* of the word, but they do not alter its spelling when they are added.

The negative prefixes **un-**, **dis-**, **mis-**, and **non-** mean "not" or "without."

unhappy	**mis**understand
disagree	**non**fiction

The prefix **in-** also means "not" in many cases. It is used before most consonants and vowels, but it changes to **im-** before words beginning with *m* or *p*; to **il-** before words beginning with *l*; and to **-ir** before words beginning with *r*. These are called *absorbed prefixes* (or *assimilated prefixes*).

incorrect	**im**patient
inactive	**il**legible
inexpensive	**ir**regular

Prefixes can also be added to **word roots.** These are word parts that have been taken into English from other languages. (See page 62 for more information on **Roots.**) The Latin prefixes *com-* and *ad-* are often joined with Latin roots, as you will see in the following examples.

The Latin prefix **com**- means "with." It is used before roots beginning with *b*, *m*, or *p*.

combine	**com**mit
compare	**com**municate
compete	**com**mand

This prefix changes to **col**- before roots beginning with *l* and to **con**- before all other letters.

collapse	**con**nect
collect	**con**duct
collide	**con**fuse
collaborate	**con**tinue

The Latin prefix **ad**- means "to" or "toward." It changes to *ac*, *af*-, *ap*-, *as*-, or *at*- when it is absorbed by the roots that follow it.

admire	**ad**mit
accept	**ac**cident
affect	**af**flict
appear	**ap**ply
assign	**as**sume
attempt	**at**tract

The prefixes *de-*, *dis-*, and *re-* are used to remove something or to reverse the action of a verb:

decontrol	**dis**agree	**un**lock
decompress	**dis**connect	**un**pack

Some prefixes refer to time:

pre- means "before": precede, prehistoric
fore- also means "before": forecast, foretell
re- often means "again": rewrite, recapture

Some prefixes indicate direction or location:

> *pro*- means "forward" or "before": proceed, propel
>
> *re*- often means "back": recover, retrieve
>
> *super*- means "over" or "above": supervisor, superhuman
>
> *sub*- means "under" or "below": submarine, subtract
>
> This prefix changes to *sup*- before the letter *p*: support, supply

The following prefixes also refer to direction:

> *ex*- means "from" or "out of": exit, export
>
> *in*- often means "into": include, insert
>
> > This prefix changes to *im*- before *m* or *p:* immerse, import
>
> *inter*- means "between": interval, intermediate
>
> *extra*- means "beyond": extraordinary

The following prefixes specify numbers or quantities:

> *uni*- (one): uniform, unite
>
> *bi*- (two): bicycle, bimonthly
>
> *tri*- (three): triangle, triplets
>
> *quart*- (four): quarter, quartet
>
> *dec*- (ten): decade, decathlon
>
> *cent*- (one hundred): century, centipede
>
> *semi*- (half; partly): semicircle, semiannual

- **Prepositions** are function words that show how *nouns* and *pronouns* are related to other words in the sentence.

These prepositions are most often used:

above	between	into
after	by	of
along	down	off
around	during	on
at	except	over
before	for	to
behind	from	under
beside	in	with

A **prepositional phrase** is a group of words that begins with a preposition and ends with a noun or pronoun.

> We went ***to** a movie* last night.
> The lawn mower is ***in** the garage*.
> I left a message ***for** them **at** the office*.
> Will you go ***with** me*?

Remember that **phrases** are groups of two or more related words that form *part* of a sentence. A phrase does *not* contain its own subject and predicate.

The object of the preposition is the noun or pronoun that comes at the end of a prepositional phrase. It is the word which the preposition relates to other words in the sentence.

In the following sentences, the prepositional phrases are in italics and the **object of the preposition** is in boldface.

> She lives *in a **town*** nearby.
> The beginning *of this **story*** is very scary.
> They sent a package *to **us*** last week.

Whenever you write a prepositional phrase that ends with a *pronoun*, remember to use the **object** form of the pronoun.

OBJECT PRONOUNS

	Singular	**Plural**
First person:	me	us
Second person:	you	you
Third person:	him	them
	her	
	it	

Prepositional phrases may be used as adjectives

A complete prepositional phrase can be used as an adjective to modify a noun.

The stamps *in this album* are very valuable.

The library *in my school* has many books *about sports*.

The words in italics are examples of **adjective phrases**: prepositional phrases that are used as adjectives.

Prepositional phrases may be used as adverbs

A complete prepositional phrase can also be used as an adverb. Usually these phrases modify verbs.

We left *before* the storm.

I found my boots *in* the attic.

The words in italics are examples of **adverb phrases:** prepositional phrases that are used as adverbs. In the first sentence, the phrase *before the storm* tells **when** something happened. In the second sentence, the phrase *in the attic* tells **where** something was found.

Ending sentences with a preposition

Prepositional phrases usually begin with a preposition and end with a noun or pronoun. However, in everyday writing and conversation we sometimes use sentences that place the preposition at the *end* of a sentence.

I don't know what he was talking *about*.
Is this material easy to work *with*?

It is all right to end a sentence with a preposition *if* this makes the sentence clear.

Questions that begin with *wh-* words often place the preposition at the end.

What were they talking **about**?

Which book are you looking **for**?

Whom were you talking **to**?

Whom was she waiting **for**?

The last two sentences could also be written this way:

To *whom* were you talking?
For *whom* was she waiting?

Be sure to use the object pronoun *whom* as the object of the preposition.

- A **pronoun** is a word that takes the place of a noun or nouns.

Personal pronouns take the place of nouns that name *people* and sometimes *things*. Personal pronouns may be used as *subjects* or *objects*, and each form has its own spelling pattern.

Subject pronouns are personal pronouns that can be used as **subjects** in sentences.

	SUBJECT PRONOUNS	
	Singular	**Plural**
First person	I	we
Second person	you	you
Third person	he, she, it	they

- **First person** pronouns refer to the person who is **speaking** (*I*, *we*).

- The **second person** pronoun refers to the person who is **spoken to** (*you*).

- **Third person** pronouns refer to the person or thing that is **spoken about** (*he, she, it, they*).

Object pronouns are personal pronouns that tell *who* or *what* received the action of the verb. Object pronouns are also often used after words such as *to, for,* and *with.*

OBJECT PRONOUNS

	Singular	Plural
First person	me	us
Second person	you	you
Third person	him, her, it	them

Antecedents are nouns or groups of words that are replaced by pronouns. The antecedent usually comes early in the sentence; then the pronoun comes later and refers to the antecedent. In the following examples the **antecedent** is in boldface. The *pronoun* that refers to the antecedent is in italics.

Sue and Kim saw that movie, and *they* said it was great.

My dog is very lazy, but *he* is fun to play with.

Possessive pronouns show that something belongs to someone. These pronouns *do not* add inflections, as possessive nouns do. Instead, possessive pronouns have special spellings of their own.

33

▼ When possessive pronouns are used directly before nouns, they are spelled this way:

**Possessive Pronouns
Used with Nouns**

First person	my	our
Second person	your	your
Third person	his, her, its	their

Where is **my** book?
Are these **your** rattlesnakes?
They let **their** pet alligator out to play.

▼ Possessive nouns can also be used by themselves to refer to an antecedent:

**Possessive Pronouns
That Stand Alone**

First person	mine	ours
Second person	yours	yours
Third person	his, hers, its	theirs

These carrots are **mine**.
I thought those books were **yours**.
Are these turnips **ours** or **theirs**?

Who, *whom,* **and** *whose* are pronouns that are used in specific ways:

▼ **Who** is used only as a **subject pronoun**. It is often used as the first word in an interrogative sentence.
   Who wants some more spinach and
      broccoli?

▼ **Whom** is used only as an **object pronoun**. It is often used after prepositions such as *to*, *for*, and *with*.
   To **whom** were you speaking?

▼ **Whose** is a possessive pronoun that usually comes just before a noun.
   Whose skateboard is in the bathtub?

Don't confuse the pronoun *whose* with *who's*, which is the contraction of *who is*.

Indefinite pronouns refer to people or things in general, not to specific people or places or things. The meaning of these words is made clear by context.

Most of these pronouns are singular and take the singular form of the verb, usually ending with *s* or *es* in the third person. A few may be plural and take the plural form of the verb. In the following lists, words marked with an asterisk (*) may be either singular or plural.

▼ Pronouns that refer to *all* or *every:*

everyone	everybody
either	everything
each	all *

Everyone *is* present and accounted for.
All of the ice cream *is* gone.
All of the people *are* eager to leave.

▼ Pronouns that refer to *some:*

		Plural Only	
someone	somewhere	both	few
somebody	something	many	several
some *	enough *		
more *	most *		

Someone *is* making a lot of noise.
Both of the cars *are* very rusty.
Some of the flowers *are* wilting.
Some of the paint *is* running.

▼ Pronouns that refer to *any*:
anyone   anything
anybody   anywhere
any *

Anyone *is* welcome to try.
Anybody *has* a chance to win.
Any of these pencils *are* good enough.
Any of the contestants *is* capable of
    winning.

▼ Pronouns that refer to *none:*
nobody   nothing
neither   no one
nowhere   none *

Nobody *is* at home now.
None of the money *is* missing from the safe.
None of the students *are* on the bus yet.

Demonstrative pronouns are used to *point out* something. These pronouns can be used alone and do not require an antecedent.

	Singular	Plural
To point out something close by:	this	these
To point out something far away:	that	those

This is the book I was looking for.
These are just the boots I've always wanted.

That is the place we visited last summer.
Those are the canoes we can rent.

Reflexive pronouns refer to a noun or another pronoun that has already been used in a sentence. Reflexive pronouns are used as **objects**.

REFLEXIVE PRONOUNS

Singular	**Plural**
1. myself	ourselves
2. yourself	yourselves
3. himself	themselves
herself	
itself	

I taught *myself* how to use a computer.

He prided *himself* on his work.

She bought a new coat for *herself*.

Notice the spelling of the third person pronouns *himself* and *themselves* (not *hisself* and *theirselves*).

Intensive pronouns are the same words that were listed as reflexive pronouns. However, intensive pronouns are used only to give added emphasis to another noun or pronoun. These pronouns are *not* used as objects.

I *myself* will finish the job.
I will do it *myself*.
She *herself* was the first to figure it out.
They completed the project *themselves*.

- A **sentence** is a group of words that expresses a complete thought.

The most important parts of the sentence are the *subject* and the *predicate*.

The **subject** is the part of the sentence that tells *who* or *what* the sentence is about. The subject is usually the person or thing or idea that is discussed in the sentence.

Several of my friends gave me a surprise party.

The **predicate** is the part of the sentence that says something about the subject. The predicate explains what the subject does or what it is. The predicate includes the **verb** and any other words needed to complete the meaning of the sentence.

Several of my friends gave me a surprise party.

Declarative sentences make statements. In a declarative sentence, the **subject** usually appears near the beginning and is followed by the **predicate**. A **period (.)** is used at the end of a declarative sentence.

I went to Yellowstone National Park last summer.

Interrogative sentences ask questions. In many interrogative sentences, one part of the **verb** often appears at the beginning and is followed by the **subject**. Other interrogative sentences begin with words such as *who, what, when, why,* or *how.* A **question mark (?)** is used at the end of an interrogative sentence.

> Have you ever been to Yellowstone National Park?
> When are we going to leave?

Imperative sentences tell or ask someone to do something. The word *imperative* means "having the power to direct." In an imperative sentence, the subject is usually understood because the command or request is made directly to someone. Imperative sentences usually begin with the verb or with a word such as *please.* A **period (.)** is used a the end of an imperative sentence.

> See who is at the door.
> Please close the windows before you leave.

Exclamatory sentences make strong statements of surprise or fear or excitement or other feeling. An **exclamation mark (!)** is used at the end of an exclamatory sentence.

> I couldn't believe he actually did that!

The **simple subject** tells exactly *who* is doing something or *what* the sentence is about.

> Several **students** in my class went on a trip.
> Last night's **storm** caused a lot of damage.

The **complete subject** contains all the words in the subject part of the sentence. This includes the *simple subject* as well as any other words that make the subject complete.

> **Several students in my class** went on a trip.
> **Last night's storm** caused a lot of damage.

The **simple predicate** tells exactly what the subject is or is doing. The simple predicate is the **verb**, which may contain one word or several words.

> The horses **trotted** around the track.
> The skydivers **were practicing** yesterday.
> We **will leave** for California tomorrow.

The **complete predicate** contains all the words in the predicate part of the sentence. This includes the **verb** and all the other words needed to complete the meaning of the sentence.

> After school I **went to the park near my house.**

Compound subjects contain two or more **simple subjects**, usually joined by a word such as *and* or *or*.

> **Rain** and **snow** fell all during the night.
> **Fred**, **Ginger**, and **I** are good friends.
> **Bill** or his **brother** will meet us after school.

Compound predicates contain two or more **simple predicates**, usually joined by a word such as *and*.

> We **slipped**, **slid**, and **fell** in the mud.
> I **ran** after him and **gave** him the message.

Simple sentences contain one **subject** and one **predicate**. The simple sentence expresses one complete thought.

> Mike and I | watched a rotten movie on TV last night.

Compound sentences contain two or more **simple sentences**. These simple sentences are usually connected by words such as *and, but,* or *or.* Compound sentences express two or more related thoughts.

▼ Compound sentences can show a relationship between two or more ideas:
We looked all over the place for my frog, **and** we finally found it under the couch.

▼ Compound sentences can show contrast:
I thought the rake was in the basement, **but** it was in the garage.

▼ Compound sentences can offer a choice:
You can have more pizza now, **or** you can wait until it gets even colder.

Sentence complements are words or groups of words that come after the verb in the predicate of the sentence. These words *complete* the meaning of the sentence. Sentences may contain **subject complements** or **object complements**.

Subject complements are used after linking verbs to tell more about the subject of the sentence.

Subject complements include **predicate nouns and pronouns, predicate adjectives**, and **predicate adverbs**.

▼ **Predicate nouns and pronouns** are used after linking verbs to tell what the subject of the sentence *is*. (See page 53.)

My friend is the best **pitcher** on the team.

The leader of the group was **she**.

▼ **Predicate adjectives** are used after linking verbs to modify the subject of the sentence. They give additional information about the subject.

That boulder is **enormous**.

The movie was **loud** and **exciting**.

▼ **Predicate adverbs** are used after linking verbs to tell *where* the subject of the sentence is or what *condition* it is in.

Our guests were **here** for three days.

He is usually **late** for everything.

Object complements are used after action verbs to receive the action of the verb.

Object complements include **direct objects** and **indirect objects**.

▼ **Direct objects** are nouns or pronouns that receive the action of transitive verbs.

I threw the **ball** as far as I could.

We watched **them** running in the field.

▼ **Indirect objects** are nouns or pronouns that tell *to whom* or *for whom* the action of the verb is done. Sentences containing an indirect object must also contain a direct object. The indirect object always comes *before* the direct object.
We gave **Ellen** a surprise party.
They gave **us** a ride home.

Clauses are groups of words that contain their own subject and predicate.

▼ **Independent clauses** (also called *main clauses*) are complete and make sense by themselves.
We were in a hurry to leave.

▼ **Dependent clauses** (also called *subordinate clauses*) are **not** complete and do not make sense by themselves.
. . . before the storm began.

This clause has a subject (*storm*) and a verb (*began*), but the subordinating conjunction *before* makes this a dependent clause. In order to make sense, it must be joined with an independent clause:

We were in a hurry to leave **before the storm began**.

Now the independent clause (*We were in a hurry to leave*) has been joined with the dependent clause (*before the storm began*) to form a *complex sentence*.

Complex sentences contain an independent clause and at least one dependent clause. In the following complex sentences, the dependent clause is written in boldface:

> **Because the game lasted so long,** we were late getting back home.
> We stopped playing **because a bad storm blew up.**

Appositives are nouns that are placed just after another noun to give more information about it. In the following sentence, the appositive *president* tells more about the subject, *Thomas Jefferson*.

> Thomas Jefferson, *the third **president** of the United States*, wrote the Declaration of Independence.

An **appositive phrase** contains the appositive itself as well as the other words that modify it. In the preceding sentence, the appositive phrase contains all the words in italics.

When the appositive is absolutely vital to the meaning of the sentence, it should *not* be set off by commas.

> The word ***menu*** is from the French language.

Sentence fragments are incomplete sentences that lack one or more important words. Often the subject or the verb is missing from a sentence fragment. To correct sentence fragments, add the missing words or join the fragment to other clauses to make complete sentences.

In the following examples, the sentence fragments are written in italics:

We took a trip to Disneyland. *Then to Las Vegas.*
I like action movies. *Because they are exciting.*

In the first example, the fragment lacks a subject and predicate. The second example contains a dependent clause that is written to look like a separate sentence.

Here are some ways to correct these examples. The changes are written in boldface.

We took a trip to Disneyland. Then **we went** to Las Vegas.
We took a trip to Disneyland**, and** then **we went** to Las Vegas.
I like action movies **b**ecause they are exciting.

In the last example we simply removed the period after *movies* and continued with *because* to write a complex sentence.

Run-on sentences result when individual sentences are written without clear punctuation to separate them. To correct run-on sentences, either write shorter individual sentences or join the parts of the sentence with a conjunction to form compound sentences.

Here is a run-on sentence followed by three corrected versions:

We went on vacation last month we traveled through four states we had a lot of fun.

We went on vacation last month. We traveled through four states. We had a lot of fun.

We went on vacation last month, and we traveled through four states. We had a lot of fun.

We went on vacation last month. We traveled through four states, and we had a lot of fun.

Comma faults result when a comma is used between two separate sentences. This creates a run-on sentence:

The movie was great, I liked it a lot.

The comma is a punctuation mark that is used only *within* a sentence; it does not connect or separate complete sentences. Here are two ways to correct the preceding run-on sentence:

The movie was great. I liked it a lot.
The movie was great, **and** I liked it a lot.

• **Suffixes** are syllables added to the *end* of words: *teacher*, *payment*, *assistant*, *collection*.

Suffixes allow words to be used as different parts of speech. They usually do not change the basic meaning of the word. Sometimes the spelling of the base word must be changed when suffixes are added (*receive, reception*).

▼ Many suffixes are used to create **nouns**. They are often added to base words that are verbs:

teach	teach**er**
govern	govern**or**; govern**ment**
act	act**or**; act**ion**
occupy	occup**ant**
attend	attend**ance**
hero	hero**ism**
copy	copy**ist**

▼ Other suffixes are used to form **adjectives**:

luck	luck**y**
brother	brother**ly**
break	break**able**
base	bas**ic**
child	child**ish**
beauty	beauti**ful**
create	creat**ive**

47

▼ A few suffixes are used to form **verbs**:
graduate, locate, vibrate
sharpen, quicken, moisten
beautify, justify, terrify
criticize, stabilize, apologize

SYNONYMS

• **Synonyms** are words that have the same or almost the same meaning.

big, large	cold, frigid	answer, reply
close, shut	try, attempt	thin, skinny

VERBS

- A **verb** is a word that tells what the subject of the sentence *is* or what it is *doing*. Verbs express actions or help to make statements complete.

Verbs are often used in their base forms. A **base word** is the form of the word as it is spelled before any endings are added or other changes are made. This form gives the basic meaning of the verb: *hear, run, watch, fly, think, go, jump.*

Action verbs tell what the subject of the sentence is doing: *throw, hit, see, read,* and *write* for example.

Tense refers to the form of the verb that tells *when* the action takes place. The three most basic tenses are these:

▼ **Present Tense** tells about things that are happening at the time the sentence is written or spoken. The present tense is also used to tell about things that happen over and over again.
  I *play* basketball every afternoon after school.

▼ **Past Tense** tells about things that have already happened and are completed.
  I *played* football last Saturday.

▼ **Future Tense** tells about things that will happen at some time in the future.
  I *will play* baseball when the weather is better.

Regular verbs follow certain basic patterns to form the present, past, and future tenses. The patterns are these:

Present tense: The base form of the verb is used with the first and second person singular and with all plural subjects. In the third person singular, the inflection *s* is added to most verbs.

Present Tense

First person:	I look	we look
Second person:	you look	you look
Third person:	he look**s**	they look
	she look**s**	
	it look**s**	

The inflection *es* is used in the third person singular with verbs that end with *ss, sh, ch, tch,* and *x*: *guesses, wishes, punches, catches,* and *fixes.*

First person:	I push	we push
Second person:	you push	you push
Third person:	he push**es**	they push
	she push**es**	
	it push**es**	

Past tense: The inflection *ed* is added to the base form of the verb.

Past Tense

First person:	I looked	we looked
Second person:	you looked	you looked
Third person:	he looked	they looked
	she looked	
	it looked	

Use of the *ed* inflection in the past tense is the most significant characteristic of *regular verbs*.

Future Tense: The helping verb *will* is added before the base form of the main verb.

Future Tense

First person:	I will look	we will look
Second person:	you will look	you will look
Third person:	he will look	they will look
	she will look	
	it will look	

Irregular verbs do *not* follow the patterns given for regular verbs. The most noticeable difference is in the *past tense*, in which irregular verbs do not add *ed*.

The most important irregular verb is *be*, as it is spelled in its base form.

Present Tense

First person:	I am	we are
Second person:	you are	you are
Third person:	he is	they are
	she is	
	it is	

Past Tense

First person:	I was	we were
Second person:	you were	you were
Third person:	he was	they were
	she was	
	it was	

Future Tense

First person:	I will be	we will be
Second person:	you will be	you will be
Third person:	he will be	they will be
	she will be	
	it will be	

Another important irregular verb is *have.*

Present Tense

First person:	I have	we have
Second person:	you have	you have
Third person:	he has	they have
	she has	
	it has	

Past Tense

First person:	I had	we had
Second person:	you had	you had
Third person:	he had	they had
	she had	
	it had	

Future Tense

First person:	I will have	we will have
Second person:	you will have	you will have
Third person:	he will have	they will have
	she will have	
	it will have	

Main verbs tell exactly what action the subject is taking or exactly what the subject is.

> He *runs* every evening for exercise.
> She *knows* more about computers than I do.
> They *wait* for the bus every morning.
> She *was* the best swimmer on the team.

Helping verbs come *before* main verbs and help to tell *when* the action of the verb takes place.

The helping verb *will* is used with the base form of the main verb in the **future tense**:

> We *will go* to California next summer.

The verbs *be* and *have* are also often used as helping verbs.

> I *am going* to visit my grandparents.
> They *are planning* to leave tomorrow.
> We *have seen* that movie three times.
> She *has worked* in the yard all afternoon.

Linking verbs tell what the subject of the sentence *is*, not what it *does*. Linking verbs connect the subject with additional information in the predicate. The verb *be* is the most important linking verb. Other verbs such as *seem*, *appear*, and *feel* can be used as linking verbs.

> He *is* the mayor of our town.
> She *was* my teacher last year.
> They *seemed* very tired after their long walk.

Predicate nouns and pronouns come after linking verbs and complete the meaning of the sentence. These nouns or pronouns tell what the subject *is*.

> Mr. Flernish is my baseball *coach*.
> Wanda is my best *friend*.
> The big winner in the contest was *he*.

Direct objects are nouns or pronouns that *receive* the action of a verb. Direct objects appear in the predicate of the sentence and complete the meaning of the sentence. They answer the question *what* or *whom* after an action verb.

> The batter hit *what?* The batter hit the **ball**.
> (*Ball* is the direct object; it tells what the batter hit.)
>
> We saw *whom?* We saw **them**.
> (*Them* is the direct object; it tells whom we saw.)

A **transitive verb** is an *action verb* that is followed by a direct object. The direct object is a noun or pronoun that receives the action of the verb.

Some verbs would not make sense without a direct object:

> I **threw** . . .
> We **saw** . . .
> They **pushed** . . .

The boldfaced words are **transitive verbs** that must be followed by objects that tell *who* or *what* received the action of each verb.

> I **threw** the *ball* farther than anyone else.
>
> We **saw** *them* at the fair.
>
> They **pushed** the stalled *car* to the side of the road.

An **intransitive verb** is an *action verb* that is **not** followed by a direct object. Intransitive verbs may be followed by words that tell *when* or *how* an action takes place, but they are not followed by words that answer the question **what?** or **whom?**

> I **studied** hard all day yesterday.
> They could not **see** very well in the fog.

Indirect objects are nouns or pronouns that tell *to whom/what* or *for whom/what* an action is done. Indirect objects are used *only* with transitive verbs.

Indirect objects are in boldface in these sentences:

> The teacher showed **my class** a movie about snakes.
> We gave **our team** a big pep rally.
> My parents gave **me** a new bike.
> The coach showed **us** how to catch ground balls.

- If a sentence contains an indirect object, it *must* also contain a direct object.
- The indirect object always comes *before* the direct object in declarative sentences.

Verb phrases contain a *main verb* and one or more *helping verbs.*

▼ The **main verb** expresses the most important action in the sentence. It tells exactly what the subject *is* or what it is *doing.*

▼ The **helping verb** is another verb that works with the main verb. The helping verb can show that an action will happen in the future. It can also show that an action has been completed in the past or is continuing at the present.

Here are some **declarative sentences** that use verb phrases:

> She *is looking* for a scarf to match her coat.
> They *have finished* repairing the road.
> He *will arrive* tomorrow morning.

If we want to ask a question, we can often do this by changing the order of words in the verb phrase. The helping verb is placed before the subject, and the main verb appears after the subject. These are now **interrogative sentences**:

> *Is* she *looking* for a scarf to match her coat?
> *Have* they *finished* repairing the road?
> *Will* he *arrive* tomorrow morning?

Principal parts of the verb are the four basic forms of each verb. All verb tenses are formed with these principal parts:

Present	Present Participle	Past	Past Participle
talk	(is) talking	talked	(has) talked

With regular verbs, the **present participle** ends with *ing* and is used with the helping verb *be* in its various forms:

I *am going* to visit my aunt.
We *are looking* for four-leaf clovers.
Dad *is talking* to my grandfather on the phone now.
She *was working* in the yard when we arrived.
They *were traveling* in their new van last summer.

With regular verbs, the **past participle** ends with *ed* and is used with the helping verbs *have, has,* and *had*:

We *have called* everyone on the list.
Mom *has talked* to my grandmother.
They *had collected* rare books for years.

The present participle is used to form the *present progressive,* and the past participle is used to form the *past progressive* .

The **present progressive** tells about actions that are continuing at the time they are described. It is a verb phrase that begins with a form of the helping verb *be* in the *present tense.* This helping verb is followed by the *present participle* of the main verb: *I am walking, you are looking, she is leaving, they are driving.*

The **past progressive** tells about actions that began in the past and continued for some time. It is a verb phrase that begins with a form of the helping verb *be* in the *past tense*. This helping verb is followed by the *present participle* of the main verb: *I was walking, you were looking, she was leaving, they were driving.*

The **perfect tenses** combine a form of the helping verb *have* with the *past participle* of the main verb.

The three perfect tenses are the **present perfect**, the **past perfect**, and the **future perfect**.

The **present perfect tense** combines the helping verb *have* in the present tense with the past participle of the main verb: *I have walked, you have looked, she has finished,* and so on.

The present perfect tense is used to express actions that happened at some time in the past or that began in the past and continue in the present.

The **past perfect tense** combines the helping verb *have* in the past tense with the past participle of the main verb: *I had walked, you had looked, she had finished,* and so on.

The past perfect tense is used to express an action that was completed *before* something else happened.

The **future perfect tense** combines the helping verbs *will* and *have* with the past participle of the main verb: *I will have looked, you will have walked, she will have finished.*

The future perfect tense is used to express actions that will be completed before some other action takes place in the future.

Irregular verbs do not follow the patterns used by regular verbs in the four parts of speech. In particular, irregular verbs do not add the inflection *ed* to form the past tense.

Earlier you saw the important irregular verbs *be* and *have*. Listed below are some other irregular verbs.

The principal parts of irregular verbs: I

In this group of irregular verbs, the spelling is the same in the **past tense** and the **past participle**:

Verb	Present Participle	Past	Past Participle
bring	(is) bringing	brought	(has) brought
buy	(is) buying	bought	(has) bought
catch	(is) catching	caught	(has) caught
have	(is) having	had	(has) had
leave	(is) leaving	left	(has) left
make	(is) making	made	(has) made
say	(is) saying	said	(has) said
set	(is) setting	set	(has) set
sit	(is) sitting	sat	(has) sat
teach	(is) teaching	taught	(has) taught
think	(is) thinking	thought	(has) thought

The principal parts of irregular verbs: II

In this group of irregular verbs, a different spelling is used in all the principal parts in most instances. A few verbs (such as *come* and *run*) retain the same spelling in the base form and in the past participle.

Verb	Present Participle	Past	Past Participle
be	(is) being	was	(has) been
break	(is) breaking	broke	(has) broken
choose	(is) choosing	chose	(has) chosen
come	(is) coming	came	(has) come
do	(is) doing	did	(has) done
drink	(is) drinking	drank	(has) drunk
eat	(is) eating	ate	(has) eaten
give	(is) giving	gave	(has) given
go	(is) going	went	(has) gone
run	(is) running	ran	(has) run
see	(is) seeing	saw	(has) seen
sing	(is) singing	sang	(has) sung
swim	(is) swimming	swam	(has) swum
take	(is) taking	took	(has) taken
throw	(is) throwing	threw	(has) thrown

Verbals are verb forms that are used as *other* parts of speech, not as verbs. The three major types of verbals are **infinitives**, **participles**, and **gerunds**.

▼ **Infinitives** are verb forms that can be used as *nouns*. Infinitives usually combine the word *to* with the base form of a verb: *to run, to see, to look*. **To run** in the marathon was Ed's greatest wish.

▼ **Infinitive phrases** contain the infinitive and the other words that are needed to make the meaning complete. **To win** *the state championship* was the team's goal.

▼ **Participles** can be used as *adjectives*. Both the *present participle* and the *past participle* may be used this way.
   Running water flowed over the rocks.
   Burned toast does not taste very good.

▼ **Participial phrases** include the participle and all the other words needed to complete its meaning.
   The clothes **hanging** *in the closet* need to be cleaned.
   All the books **chosen** *for this class* are very interesting.

▼ **Gerunds** are verb forms that add *ing* to the base form of the verb. Gerunds are used as *nouns*.
   Swimming is her favorite sport.
   I enjoy **hiking** and horseback **riding**.

In the first sentence the gerund *swimming* is the subject. In the second sentence, *hiking* and *riding* are objects.

▼ **Gerund phrases** include the gerund and all the other words needed to complete its meaning.
   Riding *a bike* is a lot of fun.
   Moving *all our furniture* was a difficult task.

Base words are complete words that make sense by themselves. They give the essential meaning of the word and the spelling before any endings are added or other changes are made. Most singular nouns are base words: *book, house, map, car*. Most verbs in the first person singular are also base words: *run, look, see, walk*.

Roots are word parts that originated in other languages and were taken into English in past centuries. Roots are not used independently in English; they must be combined with other word parts to form complete English words. Many roots have been taken from the Latin and Greek languages.

> The word *educate* is built on the root *duc-*, from the Latin word *ducere* (to lead, to guide).
> The word *biology* is built on roots from two Greek words: *bios* (life, way of living), and *logos* (word, speech; theory or science).

Affixes are syllables added to the beginning or the end of base words or roots. Affixes are not words in their own right, but they can affect the meaning of the base word. They often form new words that are used as different parts of speech. The basic types of affixes are **prefixes** and **suffixes**.

Prefixes are affixes added to the *beginning* of words: **un**happy, **dis**like, **mis**behave, and so on. Prefixes change the meaning of the word to which they are added, but they do not change the spelling of the word. See the separate entry for **Prefixes** in this Handbook.

Suffixes are affixes added to the *end* of words: teach**er**, pay**ment**, assist**ant**, collect**ion**, and so on. Suffixes usually retain the essential meaning of the words to which they are added, but they allow these words to be used as different parts of speech. Sometimes the spelling of the base word must be changed when suffixes are added (*receive, reception*). See the separate entry for **Suffixes** in this Handbook.

Punctuation Guide

APOSTROPHE (')

- The apostrophe is used to create possessive nouns that show who owns something.

▼ **Singular possessive nouns** end with the apostrophe and the letter *s* (*'s*).
   One *student's* composition won a prize.
   This *writer's* latest book is very good.
   The *box's* contents remained a mystery.

▼ **Plural possessive nouns** usually add only an apostrophe at the end of the regular plural form. This is because most plural nouns already end with *s* or *es*.
   Most of the *students'* papers were finished on time.
   Several of the *writers'* books won awards.
   Three of the *boxes'* labels were illegible.

▼ A few **irregular plural nouns** do not end with s. With these plural nouns, add 's to form the possessive.
All of the *women's* coats are in the closet.
The *people's* views were expressed at the meeting.
Some *children's* parents met them after school.

> • Apostrophes are also used with verbs to create contractions that combine two words into one. The apostrophe takes the place of the letter or letters left out of one of the words.

▼ **Contractions** often consist of a verb followed by the adverb *not*. An apostrophe usually takes the place of the *o* in *not* when these words are written as contractions.

don't (do not)	can't (can not)
isn't (is not)	wasn't (was not)
aren't (are not)	weren't (were not)
haven't (have not)	hadn't (had not)
doesn't (does not)	wouldn't (would not)
didn't (did not)	couldn't (could not)
won't (will not)	shouldn't (should not)

When *can not* is written as a contraction, the apostrophe takes the place of the first two letters in *not*. Also notice that *will not* changes to *won't* when it is written as a contraction.

▼ Contractions may involve a pronoun followed by the shortened form of a verb. The verbs *be, have,* and *will* are often used in contractions of this type. The apostrophe takes the place of one or two letters in each of these verbs.

I'm (I am)   we're (we are)
you're (you are)   they're (they are)
he's (he is)   she's (she is)
it's (it is)

I've (I have)   we've (we have)
you've (you have)   they've (they have)
he's (he has)   she's (she has)
it's (it has)

I'd (I had)   we'd (we had)
you'd (you had)   they'd (they had)
he'd (he had)   she'd (she had)
it'd (it had)

I'll (I will)   we'll (we will)
you'll (you will)   they'll (they will)
he'll (he will)   she'll (she will)
it'll (it will)

▼ Contractions can be formed by shortening the verb after interrogative pronouns (*who, what*) and after adverbs that introduce questions (*how, when, where*). The verbs *be* and *will* are often used this way.

How's it going? (**How is** it going?)
Who's at the door? (**Who is** at the door?)
What's the answer? (**What is** the answer?)
When's he going to meet us? (**When is** he going to meet us?)
Where's my other glove? (**Where is** my other glove?)
Who'll pick me up? (**Who will** pick me up?)
What'll I do then? (**What will** I do then?)

▼ Sometimes a verb can be joined with a noun to form a contraction. The verb *be* is often used this way.

Ellen's going with us. (**Ellen is** going with us.)

Ed's working in the yard. (**Ed is** working in the yard.)

The **dog's** chasing a squirrel. (The **dog is** chasing a squirrel.)

The words *Ellen's, Ed's,* and *dog's* look like *possessive nouns*, but notice that each noun is followed by a verb ending with *-ing*. This verb form is called the **present participle**. Verb phrases such as *is going, is working,* and *is chasing* are examples of the **present progressive**. In this form, the helping verb *be* is followed by a present participle, which provides the *main verb*.

COLON (:)

▼ The colon is used between the hour and the minute when the time is written in numbers.

It is now 10:15 a.m.

The movie starts at 7:30 p.m.

Notice that **a.m.** and **p.m.** are written with periods (not **am** and **pm**). Look at the entry for the **period** to see why this is so.

▼ The colon is used after the salutation in a formal letter.

Dear Sir or Madam:

Dear Mrs. Evans:

Dear Dr. Williams:

▼ The colon is used to introduce a list of items at the end of a sentence. Usually the beginning of the sentence will contain a phrase such as *the following*.

> Our supply closet contains the following items: four staplers, three rolls of tape, two pairs of scissors, and six boxes of paper clips.

COMMA (,)

▼ Commas are used to separate three or more items in a series.

> Snakes, turtles, and lizards are cold-blooded animals.
>
> The zoo just got some camels, zebras, elephants, and kangaroos.
>
> We went to Washington, Philadelphia, and New York.

▼ The comma should be used to separate two adjectives if both adjectives are of equal importance and if their order could be reversed.

> He can be a stubborn, difficult person.
>
> He can be a difficult, stubborn person.

Do not use a comma to separate two adjectives before a noun if the adjectives work together and if they would not make sense in reverse order.

> I found a *big brown* spider under that rock.
>
> The *little gray* mouse was hiding in the corner.

▼ Commas separate the two parts of a compound sentence. The comma is placed just before the coordinating conjunctions *and*, *or*, or *but*.

> We got the car repaired, and we completed the trip without any more problems.
>
> You can finish the ice cream now, or you can save some for later.
>
> He worked very hard, but he didn't finish before the rain started.

▼ Commas are used to set off brief introductory parts of a sentence. These are usually interjections or names used in direct address.

> Well, I'm glad that job is finished.
>
> So, you finally got here.
>
> Allen, please bring me some more ketchup.
>
> Kim, will you see who is at the door?

▼ A comma is used at the end of a *dependent clause* when it begins the sentence.

> After the storm ended, we went out to look at the damage.
>
> Before we leave, we should be sure we've got everything we will need.

EXCLAMATION MARK (!)

An exclamation mark is used at the end of an exclamatory sentence that expresses surprise or anger or some other strong feeling.

I never want to go through that again!

This room is an unbelievable mess!

An exclamation mark may also be used after an interjection at the beginning of a sentence. This helps to make the effect of the interjection stronger than it would be if a comma were used.

Ouch! That really hurt!

Oh NO! You didn't really do that, did you?

▼ The hyphen connects the parts of some compound words.

baby-sit	push-ups
great-grandmother	great-grandfather
mother-in-law	father-in-law
runner-up	by-product
merry-go-round	front-runner

▼ When compound numbers from twenty-one through ninety-nine are written out, the hyphen should be used.

thirty-two	fifty-seven
eighty-five	ninety-three

▼ When compound words are used as adjectives just before nouns, these adjectives are often hyphenated. This is especially true with adjectives beginning with the word *well*.

They are *well-known* performers.

That was a *fast-paced* movie.

When these compound adjectives appear after the noun they modify, the hyphen is not used.

They are performers who are well known.

▼ If you want to divide a long word between two lines, then use a hyphen between syllables. Words containing only one syllable are never divided, and longer words should be hyphenated according to their syllable patterns.

Some words contain doubled consonants which often appear at the end of stressed short-vowel syllables. In words of this type, place the hyphen between the consonants:

but-ter, mid-dle, col-lar, rab-bit, chal-lenge

In many other words, one syllable ends with a consonant and the next syllable begins with a different consonant. Place the hyphen between the consonants in words such as these:

lum-ber, fin-ger, spar-kle, for-tune

When one syllable ends with a long vowel and the next syllable begins with a consonant, place the hyphen between the long vowel and the consonant:

la-bor, fi-nal, no-tice, ru-mor

You know that many words begin with prefixes and end with suffixes. Place the hyphen so that the structure of the word is clear: prefix-root-suffix. When a suffix begins with a consonant, the hyphen is placed just before this consonant. When a suffix begins with a vowel, then the hyphen is often placed just before the *preceding* consonant.

in-crease, ex-press, con-clude, at-tract
use-ful, worth-less, pay-ment, kind-ness
com-mit-ment, at-trac-tion, de-pen-dent

Use your knowledge of base words and roots to help you decide how to hyphenate long words. This information, combined with your knowledge of prefixes and suffixes, will usually help you determine the logical way to hyphenate words such as these when they appear at the end of a line:

com-municate, commu-nicate, communi-cate
in-complete, incom-plete
en-chantment, enchant-ment
com-puter, comput-er

When you need to divide a long word at the end of a line, do not guess where to put the hyphen. If you are not sure, then check your dictionary.

PERIOD (.)

▼ The period is used at the end of **declarative sentences** and **imperative sentences**.
I don't know where the time went.
Please close the door when you leave.

▼ The period is used with **abbreviations** to show that some letters have been omitted from words.

Mr. (Mister)   Sun. (Sunday)
Mrs. (Mistress)   Tues. (Tuesday)
Ave. (Avenue)   Jan. (January)
St. (Street)   Nov. (November)

When we write the time we use the abbreviations **a.m.** and **p.m.**, which must always include a period after each letter: 9:15 a.m., 6:30 p.m. This is because **a.m.** is an abbreviation for the Latin words *ante meridiem* (before noon) and *p.m.* is an abbreviation for *post meridiem* (after noon).

QUESTION MARK (?)

The question mark is used at the end of **interrogative sentences**.

Where have you been?
Who was on the phone?
How much more pizza can you eat?

Quotation marks are used to show who is speaking when you write **dialogue**: a conversation between two or more people. *Quotation marks are always used in pairs.*

▼ Place one quotation mark before the first spoken word and another quotation mark after the last spoken word.

▼ The word just after the first quotation mark is always capitalized.

▼ If the spoken passage begins with words such as *He said* or *She asked*, place a comma after these words just before the first quotation mark.

▼ If the spoken passage comes at the end of the sentence, then place the end punctuation inside the quotation mark.
    He said, "I think I'd better leave now."
    She asked, "How much longer do we have to wait?"

▼ If words such as *he said* or *she said* appear after the spoken passage, then a comma is usually placed before the last quotation mark.
    "It's time to leave," he said.
    "I don't know where he is," she replied.

▼ If the spoken passage is a **question** or an **exclamation**, then the question mark or the exclamation mark is used as punctuation just before the last quotation mark. The complete sentence ends with a period.
    "Watch out for that low branch!" she shouted.
    "When will you be ready to leave?" he asked.

▼ When you write dialogue, begin a new paragraph each time the speaker changes. Also use only one set of quotation marks when one person speaks several sentences in a row.

> "When can we leave?" whined Robert.
> "We will leave when everything is ready," replied Dad.
> Mom said, "We can't leave now because I have to feed the cat and take the dog for a walk. Dad has to make sure all the windows are closed, and you still have to clean up your room."
> "Well, maybe we shouldn't plan to leave before tomorrow," said Dad as he retrieved a roller skate from the kitchen cabinet.

SEMICOLON (;)

The semicolon can be used to separate the two parts of a compound sentence. When this is done, the semicolon takes the place of a conjunction such as *and*, *or*, or *but*. The semicolon shows that the two parts of the sentence are of equal importance.

> They wanted to play baseball; I wanted to go swimming.
> Maria went to the movie; Ellen went shopping.

Notes

Notes

Notes

Special Offer!

Write or call now for your free year's
subscription to Grayson Bernard
Publishers' parent newsletter:

Parent & *Child . . . learning together*

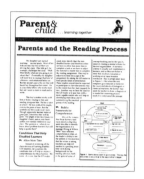

Receive four quarterly issues filled with information
and advice all concerned parents need.

Simply mail in the order form below or call
(812) 331-8182 for your free subscription.

Name _____

Address _____

City _____ Zip _____

Ages of my children _____

Topics I'd like to read about _____

Mail to:　　　Grayson Bernard Publishers
　　　　　　　Free Subscription Offer
　　　　　　　223 S. Pete Ellis Drive, Suite 12
　　　　　　　Bloomington, IN 47408

Books for Home and School
from Grayson Bernard Publishers

▼ *Grammar Handbook for Home and School*
  by Carl B. Smith, Ph.D.

  A quick reference with concise explanations of the basics of English grammar and punctuation. The perfect companion to *Intermediate Grammar.*

▼ *Intermediate Grammar: A Student's Resource Book*
  by Carl B. Smith, Ph.D.

  A student's grammatical lifesaver! Complete explanations and examples, plus a handy punctuation guide.

▼ *Elementary Grammar: A Child's Resource Book*
  by Carl B. Smith, Ph.D.

  A handy source of answers and explanations for young learners and their parents.

Create a success story with . . .

Smart Learning: A Study Skills Guide for Teens *by William Christen and Thomas Murphy*

Learn to focus study time and energy for fantastic results the whole family will be proud of!

▼ The Confident Learner: Help Your Child Succeed in School by Marjorie R. Simic, Melinda McClain, and Michael Shermis

A guide to everything from homework to high motivation—a confidence builder for both parents and children!

▼ Help Your Child Read and Succeed: A Parents' Guide by Carl B. Smith, Ph.D.

Practical, caring advice with skill-building activities for parents and children from a leading expert in the field.

▼ Expand Your Child's Vocabulary: A Twelve-Week Plan by Carl B. Smith, Ph.D.

A dozen super strategies for vocabulary growth— because word power is part of success at all stages of life.

Find these valuable resources at your favorite bookstore, or use the order form on the next page to have these books sent directly to you.

Order Information

☎ To order by phone, call toll-free 1-800-356-9315 and use your VISA, MasterCard, or American Express.

✉ To order books by mail, fill out the form below and send to

Grayson Bernard Publishers
P. O. Box 5247, Dept. GH
Bloomington, IN 47407 • (812) 331-8182

Qty.	Title	Author	Unit Cost	Total
	Grammar Handbook	Smith, C.	$ 8.95	
	Intermediate Grammar (available Fall 1992)	Smith, C.	$16.95	
	Elementary Grammar	Smith, C.	$13.95	
	Smart Learning	Christen/ Murphy	$10.95	
	The Confident Learner	Simic, M.	$ 9.95	
	Help Your Child Read and Succeed	Smith, C.	$12.95	
	Expand Your Child's Vocabulary	Smith, C.	$ 7.95	

Shipping & Handling
$3.00 for the first book plus $1.00 for each additional book.

Subtotal	
Shipping & Handling	
IN residents add 5% sales tax	
TOTAL	

Method of Payment
❏ check ❏ money order
❏ Master Card ❏ Visa

Card holder_____

Card no. _____

Expiration date _____

Send books to:

Name _____

Address _____

City_____State _____ Zip _____

Prices subject to change.

Your satisfaction is guaranteed.
Any book may be returned within 60 days for a full refund.